Luke Beesley | Aqua Spinach

New Poems

GIRAMONDO POETS

Luke Beesley | Aqua Spinach

First published 2018
from the Writing & Society Research Centre
at Western Sydney University
by the Giramondo Publishing Company
PO Box 752 Artarmon NSW 1570 Australia
www.giramondopublishing.com

Designed by Harry Williamson
Typeset by Andrew Davies
in 10/16.5 pt Baskerville

Printed and bound by Ligare

Distributed in Australia by NewSouth Books

Cataloguing-in-Publication data
is available from the
National Library of Australia

ISBN 978-1-925336-95-5 (pbk)

In the empty moment, what you call identity ceases to be continuous, linear, apparent.
It's hazy and insubstantial, a jumbled, fragmented surface.
It skips around from one time to another, from one place to another.
It refuses to respect the need to keep one moment consistent and continuous with the ones that precede or follow it.
It's a film.

LEO CHARNEY, *Empty Moments: Cinema, Modernity, and Drift*

Contents

Ink

Media

In the morning I started writing so slowly I got on a bus. My hand went away like one half of a drawbridge. It was like dreaming, after all, and I got off at the park. In the park the foreground was sharp. Little wet fonts tied a pigeon to the edge of a seesaw. Elsewhere was chaos – a mélange of radiant hue, shallow depth of field. It was impossible to walk into – sizzling colour, blurring landscape receding as I wrote towards it.

Circling

In seven minutes there will be an old phone at the windowsill of your reader's thought – you, as reader of this, or this eaten presentation. A ceramic, glazed spearmint. Actually the same colour as the telephone – the pocked receiver, a long list of expectations. We're on a bus! The wide windows, frameless, modern, surprised us. As did that finicky *B* that must have been trapped in it when boarding, its running writing looping round the bright pollen-coloured modern seating. What's the time, you might ask, and I begin all over again. Beauty! Balance! The crane crumbles along the sky like a dropped-out line. It seems to hear like a headline. How early can we contrive a whole day?

Trumpet

A story about opening a notebook to place an idea down, was one of the worst ideas. I've placed on the table. The kitchen light is the same colour as the pulpy juice – dust motes float around verb in all literature, the dust motes float. Floating dust brings to mind a tendency or the difficulty in describing affectation, the trail of thought on the mind of the writing writer. Try bringing to mind or recollect. Collect in a corner or on the corner of the mind a lettuce. Fresh as the ski lifts with the hill and powders her nose. She exists in an almost-circle of powder, pom-pom, audibly describing also the effect of a thought on the mind of the writer. It's difficult. Beneath the sound of a scratching leaf on the sill would allow later the morning light slantwise, illuminant, the foggy room's dusty remembering, is a tree. I put my finger into my ear to know. O, I know. But putting my finger into my ear I regale or recall that silly pose, recall pollen, pom and pollen, pomp! The lip at its business of embouchure (trumpet).

Billion Billion

click of the blue bic lighter

and part my timber omega on, wearing it all
shining a torch at it when outside

to trust the dishwasher
galaxy metaphor

Quiet as an Ashtray

The writer bothered himself, and then he grew kind. His kindness was of a sort, an affectation rumoured in his Proust streak. He planned to daydream in meetings and portion his day sideways into the florid collection of petals at the 'quarter past' of the plate. At three o'clock or at night. The writer broke back into his house to retrieve a collection of books that his wife was holding apart. The old tuba beheaded and placed on the wall, its opening reflected in the lamplight seemed to elongate the light. Though he compared it to an elephant, instead. His own ego – aggrieved and ornamental, now, so annoying or was it bothersome? They had a deal. She wouldn't change the locks, and he agreed to meet her sister's counsellor every other Monday afternoon and afterwards email. Her inbox filled like the street when everyone came out of their houses following news of the President's assassination.

One Eye Missing

Something as domestic as a cup of tea – knitted and besotted into so few daydreams the imagination envies the domestic, the weave of routine down the stars, through administration offices, planets beleaguered even train-related off track thoughts interrupting other minor daydreams. When all seems trivial to distracted thought, one of the workers sleeps in a cupboard simile.

Teddy Bear Lost to Peanut Butter and Eaten by the Neighbour's Doberman

Pack a fallen branch into the disco bag. Wipe its cut across your cheek, from the back of your hand, actually weeping. Go back inside in a silvery breeze edging the novel's dusty corners. And for what is a corner other than to leap with one leg sideways and follow it on another? Present! An accumulation of years kneaded out from under the eye with the windworn handle of a bell. Or it's forgotten, the beginning, until you give yourself space, wear a path on the branch, climbing. It's like a dance messed up. Or fling a few words into the trees.

The Delay

And for the last word we'll need two open pages and a book of rolled soccer plays. Say, a pass-to-pass or defence-to-striker where the ball appears mid-conversation as a little mole on the eyelid. It's flicked up and caught in the warped cube of sunlight and lost on the pure native branch which when bent to a metaphor in literature is simply an arm in science. A skeletal autumn when the leaves fall early and the window is exposed suddenly and you never notice it in ten years of a partnership when massaging a foot became a way to plant a key when she stayed overnight at her mother's after the eye op. I'm delaying the whole morning in an open patio. The sandpaper of the citrus-coloured searches new dust in the room freed in falling off the bed. I think I'd forgotten what she watched, tasted like, thinking through the menu – an instinct to brush the specialised serif price from the clipboard. I actually have a pencil blister is something I've been lazily trying to get into a conversation that I'd not had ownership over. This sentence exists to reach the last page of the exercise pad – leap! – Japanese, existing in double meaning as *e* replaces the

very last *a* in stationary.

Into this Apricot

How would you drown? I'd prefer to take the stairs. Which liquid? Milk to experience the true envelope. Ah. Your chicken burger is burning. Watch your television it will outshine you. Our faces intermingle in the static Helen Frankenthaler left on a beach. Organs pew comfort anti-joy Juan essence cycling. Riding a bike from this corner shop archaic, tic, architect cash packing canvas fruity wallet unbuttoned centrepiece to the early first show of the summer. Sprinkling of pink as Jupiter's rank stinking moons swing orbit day sky realist figurative deco nourishment for parts part tan-bark missions into forest terrain table commune filtered through cheap curtains we threw up in.

in all literature. An entire bookshelf
in the spine of a tooth.

The fading nipple
coloured coral. I play a chord. Chord.

Full Spot

Below the plain puzzled away in agitation ocean surf was also the desk. Scandinavian timber hovering birth lines characteristics eventually presented encyclopaedic graphs approximate the skittish brain motion. Little smear breathing across my right hand. One taut itch at the cheek. It's nothing more than what was erected by a breeze. Australian. Arms listed in the foliage of a backpress gym sonic. I watch a fluorescent insignia passing freight train. Above it the cloudy eyes swelter and redden and this, in my running, overt body stasis, each font on a tan page the pages folding away, beneath me, read.

Otter Waist

I leave my last line on a public bench. People move orderly past and he, peeling off the crowds, crustaceans himself and begins to read. He reads heavily with garlic cloves he spreads on a picnic table like dice. Imagine the smell of his wrists, pockets, inlet, leading indiscriminately to the sea again. Dorsal attention and the dolphin-coloured clouds slug out unopened. I release my last line. I'm in a train carriage half asleep eating cashews. At the next stop blonde hair lighting which is a form of monument which underpins nervous sunline across the platform and she reaches a commuter in a suit to rearrange the whole black straight shining style (we take years to spell it correctly). I loop back to the city. For a long time I think the line is left to dig and deliberately forget to get off and double back, again, to retrieve itself. I'm on a train. It is a great levelling fact. Another line opens out at Central and the carriage needles minor sports in an attempt to return to the only technique I shaped my seated nature to and I try to think of ways to lose the tongue in a wordless hour waiting for the train. Condensed New York on the phone ingrained arc of arm-on-tortoise, turtle-on-sunset. I fling a tattoo out dramatically and the train lurches forward, or this before that that this came before, and was solely within temperature a hazard blue lurid not long lost stomach scrunched in A4 moved a block and then unwrapped in front of an audience expecting entertainment, the train coming to a stop. I left it up the escalator and skipped stairs I would have to owe in the future but for now given the spelled circumstance pocket the prose ringing on a park bench when I found it!

Searchers

When John spoke so gently of Frank's voice his soft voice crumbed the radio waves basically O'Hara's voice was a meal, too, similar and 'gentle', 'soft', as Ashbery said. He said it with melancholy but that tone was often in his voice, a muffled satisfaction. Hidden in the floor, they skirt echidna emotions and have a break, snack. I sit down in the warm air-conditioning and try to conjure sorrow. I wear no tracksuit. Sprinting, though, I spill photographs of my childhood all over my shirt, and paper towels invade my perception of myself. When is shame's slow cunning going to walk up to a line of poetry on the street and introduce it to Ashbery who met gentle O'Hara and argued with Stevens in that old hotel and woke up shameful of his surrealist libertarian heart? What puts Frank at the heart of Wallace Stevens, exploding? John meets Frank on a dream whims like delicate logic into a cuneiform patience: his typewriter's medicinal restoration broken by 150–170 km/hour luncheons. They took five minutes to become lifelong friends, said Ashbery, in the wind, the pure static of his thinking on Heidegger, hollow imagination or nasal oppression stomach interruption/sponge or revenge. I can't keep the photocopying up. I can't. I can't wake. The light burns a hole in my eardrum clean – Western.

The Morning's Phone Chance

Unnerving latte willowing in the corner balcony hadn't dreamed cold and fifteen times further annotated at the last page of the bus up there unnoted like a shirt party. If pure beauty isn't awarded coincidence it remains clothed, hopping on a bus. Call me bus the beauty coming off the *B* is ordinarily placed in a basket to breathe and in particular time will snap like a photo.

A Century of Poetry in English

Oven pottery in the language inherited a century of prose and lilac Iliads. The Iliads by binoculars and binoculars by lower lake and the century in English against French or Spanish soccer grace, Keatsean anticlimactic brilliance, William-to-William, wheeled in on bright cuts and English lessons. The sentence flosses the Armadillo mountains in the east and the sun reaches out of atmosphere like a sneeze, centuries. We work around the spine.

Obliterated Joy

The best years of the 21st century war actually quartered thoughts chickened-up out of great gravy occurrences. Or it was a melancholic occurrence of cerebral order or shorthand, a coagulate of half thought on the boundary between Eastern thought and Eastern European picnic minded mindless congratulated punctuality. On a quarter chord of crusted worried breeze was again a pick or picked-at thinking brushed her hair – a minor favourite. Obliterated joy and the air dusted steps and fingertips which we would take for ignorant burglary. Forced mime! Incomplete crashed computer like alfoil made to cramp a rat's progress in a cupboard hole.

The Lobster

Of course André Breton named him the conquistador of
the dreamlife. Surrealism flirts on the basis of negative aroma.
Whiff and double numbers in the mucky art of pure nom-
enclature, mould on the other side of a *V* coagulated in a
little night scene in the adult hospital play. The clean pur-
pose and metre. Oh the receptionist went and he didn't
(or mind). Songs only owned or copied unnamed signatures
– oh! Flamboyant loopy *ys* (whys) polished nails the colour
of shipping containers. Call! Ah said the patient. Er went
the theory otherwise solvent afterthought.

Big Noun Sways

The small *e* I thought to dither through a party straw.

Gallery Fatigue

I ran my finger down the abridged right side of the paragraph keys, stairs, door. I knocked a few times confidently. Elizabeth Bishop opened the door and I gave her the cup of tea I'd purchased at a roadside van selling falafel kebabs. I'd waited in line for ages and she took my hand and we sat at the kitchen table with *B* in our names and drank beer. There was a silence like the texture of the snow itself. Surprisingly soft – always surprising. I can't name it. We nursed smiles or a complexion and talked about William H. Gass. A fan turned up and I squeezed her hand. She led me to the door pointed out punctuation along her roofs with a shaky finger. I saw the skin under her fingernail in the pinkyblue bottom lefthand corner of *Les Demoiselles d'Avignon*, which was gorgeous in the flesh. A real surprise.

Reunion Song

Every time she saw herself in the mirror, I remember, she pushed her chin forwards so as to stretch the skin of her neck. The crushed tram ticket in her throat produced the crumpled husky sound, itself. She had seen a throat specialist at one point and I told her a long anecdote about my trip to NY, which fanned out from the phrase 'detective work' that I used to describe my absorption in research. I sat there in the library for nine hours a day, a short lunch in the brisk sub-zero sun, and spoke to her of the blizzard and its pattern on the East Coast. A doctor pointed the sharp beak of curlew at her neck which twitched like a nerve as she sang: it's nearly ten! We had had another wine and met outside the pain – eight years. Most of the local bars were closed and the cellar was closed to the public given a whisky festival. I stirred honey into the corner of my mouth and went to scratch my own brain through a hole in the back of my skull obscured by a flap of thick hair. The texture of a soccer ball retrieved from a swamp, my mind. Colour of cross trainers, lycra. She'd been an avid runner. It's hard to communicate the evening without thinking about break-up (ours) and death (her mother's) but we used those words. The light was very low.

More on Bob Dylan's Day

They called him Dylan because he kept a harmonica along his cough. He coughed gently through his nose. His nose was the shape of half an opening silver gum wrapper and I was having a game of golf with him. We had played four days and I could already sense that a thought, itself, was beginning to distract Dylan's putting. He put it over on my niblick shoe, and I didn't flinch. The way arborists fell a tree across the yard mid-conversation already drinking tea you offered them on arrival. His swing, like that of the very tree, was nasally. I guess that's also why they called him Dylan. Bob! I yelled, that day, instead of fore! And we laughed. It's just … I couldn't bring him to a point. My sister called Dylan's dilemma a red flag but in truth many of the holes held red flags and there was no breeze at all, just a dribble either side of the pin (which I used to write this).

Buñuel's

We may have to catch the bus out of the building glistening and ascending into soft options, crowded sticky seats. So, these poems recipe themselves a bit, though I provide no insight into competition or televised hairsprayed lettuce flexing in air-conditioning. This kitchen scene is one attempt, the delight at 3.30 pm, a pew mongrel in the arch of secular air temperature. If you sit up on the sink you will, and I can show you the water runs until pipes cool and antelope tart. Tarted. It – the literature – envelopes to a raw package of sunlight inching towards the express box. Postage box we know and a friend wobbles into pregnancy. Wow! She craves sliced kites and her coffee closed on my armpit until the doors flung open and disembarked anthologies pixelated in the last few syllables of a poppy popped pop po doggy!

Paint

Stars

I worked up into a goalpost and arranged a sanding. The flakes of the plaster cast a shade on the shaved law. I placed my foot wide and the notes suggested by the umpire spakfilla-ed his thoughts with a set of gulps out of pool filter. I did another lap and the football cherished it and wound into a description of idle water. There were three players chewing swimming caps spitting blue bits into an ashtray. I couldn't walk past their glare ricocheted off the bus twisting out around the entrance. I was on the bus, on a towel, and tried to read the emergency procedure around exits (glass that crumbles in thickened frisbees). I had a retainer in my mouth and I tried to remove it. My teeth made the sound of cellophane biscuit-y light that had painted my bare, still-wet stomach bright and sticky from the pool. I asked. I asked after an airbag, or the driver's disc history, or troubling stretches of road way down towards the moon.

Top Floor

Almonds their carpentry as violins top floor and rolled up mountains delivered in alfoil. Peeling back curtains to let in the means. Antlers used as a toothpick. Image: getting atop yesterday's early morning dream of overlapping hamburger. Or the stratosphere below our ankles where bright weed flowers and circumstances leave us luggage. She fell into a four-wheel drive parking at the airport. Hips splintered further into her biography, wheeling her onto the dance floor unashamed, David Bowie, spinning her round like a steering wheel. Seatbelt impedance the car's delivery against capital meant our lips were caught in diamond intricate siren internals where the autopsy revealed earlier the blue underpainted pure white light of actual paint under microscope pale swimming pool hue. How long have we been swimming? To a wrinkle you said as if a point, or up to, and they slipped, dripping. Pollock on his birthday. Once, he walked three towns over to buy a chocolate bar. Caught an ambulance back using a severe nosebleed. The weather was lost in the car or vice versa, so all Lee Krasner saw was a sceptical ketchup pulse knocking at the kitchen window.

Doubling

I stirred and woke early, my eyelids still envelopes she posted
a thin paper airplane through the scar. A superficial glance
her hair followed. Soothe, I said. Glinting, the sunlight pasted
gluggy hesitant on the bricks and the garage door flew against
my knee. No one answered. The paper was a rickety ear against
my nose and I bit in, scooping up the lobe. Pita filled a corner
and I went into the sun to dry. Grass in sharp loose triangles
meant I had to upturn false teeth, I hadn't drawn against the red
outline of the open trampoline zipped up and spent 95% of the
time in mid-air.

Numerals in the Second Chapter

Courbet's palette knife
across pebbled beach, his reflection nursed in

turn by the open sky. I go back and highlights
during the poem.

Chrome Splinters

Beach like the following couples on a beach had the same tributary and the same umbrellas. We walked under each and the next day stepped through hedges and the soft sand down to compacted difference. Our steps had somewhat made to seal it as the leather of a drum. Pat pat. In sixteen minutes the sun would disappear waves calm and they would continue in their cached hollows and go on unknowing – trespassing, legs tangled in the wrong name.

Aquatic Centre

Truth the cabbage intercepts on its seagreen or its quick pepper-
corn only poem mirrors the aftermath of a house-warming. Walls

grub up to the tallest guests and the short gusts scrub the corners
of the first and last lines to create a cubism already departed.

Portrait

It came in beside a character reference and ricocheted nearly nine times the national debt. I was working on an ark pole. The dainty property index flickered like a little nerve. You did! And stayed long into spaghetti we ordered in Osaka and regretted it. Someone came to our table with hairspray. I tried to jerk my head in amongst it but sake tipped the fake Everest glass and I went to quietly hire a brand new Fender Jaguar. I thought I could get a line in on frequently indented facial tics which distracted my first chance at the portrait prize. I had a fuzzed brush, clogged, and my sleep was eaten by a few ants in pursuit of a dead lizard. Isn't it funny how Christmas shouldn't get home till midnight but text if the train departs late.

How to Cure a Headache

Art is its own bracket, originally of course made from a thicket. A headache taps on an area close to the ear until you offer the watermelon as piñata. The party obliges but all you can find in the garage is an old putter. You put, or it, out in the side of the guest, and they swing it around in a form, punctuation, that could only have existed in watermelon pink. I always swallow the seeds, someone says, and there is pure silence – the silence of mini blonde seeds camouflaged so completely in my headache. I can only test a thought. Parenthesis leads to historicisation when only yesterday it allowed me to remove the flesh of watermelon by crippling one half around the lip of the toilet bowl (I mutter). And yet there it is, unstable. The guests and I were lining up, stepping from foot to foot, practising the lines in our faces unmatched. I would have to be embarrassed and was immediately relieved. I noticed, also, that my headache was gone.

The Opening

I principally remember the room – artless and minor yet minimalist cultural ignorance that sold. High-five priceways ordered fastidiously from the menu as he walked in the door the sun went out of his face, as they say. Life in him was an autocratic tumble-dry. In accordance the heritage trust gave him a social air that betrayed insecurities and his domestic dislocation: he had fallen off a mule onto an expressway and it took an hour to hail someone down and set his injured shoulder. All they had was a crowbar. He watered the garden. He did extremely odd jobs (replaced putty in water features with translucent afterbirth).

Roussel's Helicopter

A helicopter at the air jogging off along an invisible line between two suburbs. It pulled up tilting forwards like a dragonfly and wobbled over the composition of a letter. I'd composed probably three-quarters of the letter almost without realising it between cups of coffee looking up at the blade and thinking yes thwacking against the sound of the helicopter. I'd avoided the *D* for some time, and it had grown into a complicated very good letter, to get us back to amicability, sunflowers in the yard, the painterly rust colours and delicate hot brush-strokes. The clothesline and its facts staring in a yellow ochre. The helicopter, writing this down, was absent.

Lucian and the *London Review* 6/6/13 p.10

Titian's genius far beyond the elbow of the rosy sitter is an open melon jewelled on narrative. His models doused in vermilion, busied? He criticised her forearm until the blood uttered, tutored sunset, avuncularly doubled or a quarter of his own genius beautiful-

ly bearded in prickly snow.

Le dejeuner sur l'herbe frame in *Un chien Andalou*

Who Manet's son/was oyster enter from a cashier of sequins trees dessert/attitudinal escort parole. He refused the amputation/indefinitely vented cane/another of the branches/disappeared the way a veil reveals a horse's true paddock/service/showhorse repeated (highlights of the canvas/siphons in clocks indent across/back radiant infatuation illegitimate) action. I think combats bathers more in common with *Le dejeuner sur l'herbe* than does clothed. Nymph/went the door knob as Foster (writer) took it into strides to minimise distractions/planet in itself on the deck/thought though putting his pencil down/singing door knob.

A Hat

I had been walking for 10–15 mins without a hat. Inside the hat I was able and I was able. Customer accounts. Phlegm of coat rack hardened around my shoulders. Amuck this gunky silvery circumstance, I made a decision, or it, it was the dec tha ma! The made, ago. Idled another coriander blemish. Awning. Team, to ever, day, docent. Soup with three full. Or stopped-up chicken cougher? *Arp*. I had been walking alongside water lilies (you can!) too! Have to(o) take me till I walked into the early 20th century and spied Arp up in the late, by it. MoMA said warm itinerary. I have it.

Dream 2

I talk well across the table. Across the table. I speak in Hindi trying untucked phrasing and she reaches over and pushes my bottom lip back into my mouth like a napkin at the shirt collar. We order egg-plant beer affogato dessert paisley sourdough eateries and some of us go to sleep under the chair for health, hegemony. My painting slips on olive oils and careens into unusual wallet anecdotes mumble away in my pocket biscuit Australian rancour.

White Lines on Pink

Tony Tuckson

I arrived by the pink barkstripped eucalyptus tree last Sunday and went straight to bed. I slept in the pink light of a eucalyptus tree. Sleeping was easy until I dreamed the bark stripped from my own pillow, owl-embroidered childhood pillow, collected in dream lichen florescent and waiting on kindling, something I could possibly trace back to a family tree, to the nomenclature of an arborist's labour. Apples while the sound of the river refused any softening. I sat close to its stereo. Woke up in pins and needles. To acknowledge the fire-place here and the fireplace in the sound of the second home of my childhood. Smoke flooded the house, the brickwork at poor angles, a shout ricocheting off the river as I made the bed and prepared breakfast simply and with turned eggs and the eye of the e.g. always drawing on emotion caused by repetition.

A Line in Still Life

Margaret Preston

Tagged ibis classification to assistant's watercolour knee,
a length, walking fawn over tap water and pencil holder architecture

we cannot forget broadsheet. But talking at the same humidity never
 moved in
avant with copper all fatigued those

constrained last words of the poem coloured in with her finger
in table water.

Landscapes

The talented passenger sat proudly on the scuffed leather blue pinched grubby, to repeat, scuffed purple sour leather bus seat and, proudly, for he was a cub, poured ambiguous pale rusty thin liquid into cub friend's painting bowl. Cub friend took it. He had two paintings the tea set disguised by the very nature of the foliage – was a forest, really – and sniffed and squeaked and overly disseminated its own oily pigment as the easel creaked below the painting at the mouth of a little forest. The ankle he sprained and winced drank more of the old mysterious turps gripped the grubby bus seat like his toggle did, his golden scarf. The driver searched her pocket for a banknote sure to keep her eyes on the youngsters, who were attempting at least three landscapes. One was a McCubbin rip, the other a Rupert Bunny mock. She was prepared to spin a cheque book and in doing so created what they, distracted, took for long jump the air beneath a hurdler, the paint scraped. Flaring running shorts were mere daubs the paint exiting brush and resting on poses of great personality! Leap notes and handwritten parts of a why. Kids! she yelled, and they flinched the brush imparting the right vermilion to bring the whole composition out of a self-consciousness they'd have to resist in early adolescence. What *does* a tree really *do?* etc.

The Beinecke Library

When I was about then, or when I went up three and grew.
I grew and grew. I was about nine or graded so I first had to split
a golf ball with an axe. It took an hour. My part was to the heart-
side that day. I was surprised to find that inside was a lover of books
and a few mangled rubber bands. We descended down the fairway
off the tee and saw something open in that artificial landscape.
I couldn't put my finger on it.

Sun on the Crutches

At the end of the party there was absolute Lego.
Pointed out.

A poor scout's biscuit flopped
atonally over his tin camping cup.

Purists out in the night
would like to recreate the *Mona Lisa*
hissed the insect.

2001

I'm sitting at the outdoor table. There is an orange caterpillar mimicking the mouth of the frangipani. Oracular notions of plaid, orange, she wore, and lay down on her side to allow the pleat its discreet iron. Like a canal line or snapping bamboo in half. Folding one eucalyptus leaf, listening. It's mid-afternoon airplane a house going up across the road the Modernist art of contentment, really. I know, but we have fallen so anxious as to irritate around one or two points e.g. housing, structure, fish in-and-against attraction, the contour of a leaf's relation to the hill, and the hill's relation to a swim.

The Weather

A hundred years ago it was repaired with a surgical glove
and analogue parts whistle past the impressionist rug.

In a half hour. Intaglio six. Public transport epoch! Ersatz
curtains. Our era, frames she bought at the chemist portrait-

ure. Set up with twigs. Cossington Smith. Piano tornado
to the sound, to the airplane mister! Twitchy light rain.

Broke

Hopper aqua aqueduct innocent and messy in his lunch, Lynch wipes the plane down with a squash ball and in the toaster we see Braque's fastidiousness. No better Braque in the idea of it breaking, so to speak, 'Braque Braque!' A cup of Hopper, pony! Show boats! In antiquity – spittle Hokusai-like displaced underarms each morning – the surface of the canvas – painterly rinsed eye of blue Hopper, string, emotive Dennis Hopper, in earnest. This afternoon he was caught in the untrimmed bush, puppy-dogged out of obsolescence and barked. There was no train but the thought of rain. No flesh like it. Thurs of a Thursday was the technique all the way thru the early 21st C.

Redraw

I can draw a doorway entrance remember the name of my old dog
password choc and jog put my arm into the field's tennis elected
personality scrapping trousers adhered to static air late 1990s again
buzzed comet conjugate as in corrugated out chirpily and set up
workshop around dufflecoated medium egg two hands playing
chicken in electrical storm redraw the poem on vision in the
reflection of the car sways metallic yellow high-vis poor weather.

Cubism in the Face of Optimism

Oppen, again, face dull and monotonously reading his line.
Another trick of phosphorescence antelope leap, leap antelope
play sides of oregano habit with spaghetti culture ruins the lazy
sliver of his block-clear poetry all through the centre of contem-
porary art's own architectural habits bulk optimism in the year's
knee-length opinion print broadsheet nostalgia interred adolescent
coming-of-age circuitry. We learn the alkaline ordinance of sealing,
of salmon-cultured lips. Eating salmon. Biting whole fancy faces
peering into this poem!

Petticoat Ticket Wins Tennis Racquet

Woefully obtuse grin like wild beetroot. Crouched at the garden we hit an ankle. Quarter ligament to phone (if your home number counts up). At Psarakos the cold outline of a mince collar split at the wedding. Milling in the dessert. August, we note (dart interjection) or lazy wine on our day – a cheer gallop. Messy photos we hadn't shown participants aqua spinach against the trucks. A juddered diving board in the crook or meek spin around on an office chair coat tone in awe dot underline believe it! Dollar sandwich. Petticoat a jejunely honest spring elope beeswax! Open the curtain with the actual sausage. Let light true honey knife cutlery direct barley rest, round and curt, livery. Horse dribble lace saw marketing. We bring these four petticoat tickets to eventually win a tennis racquet. Lesson the bridal whole, and the slope ignited the brother-in-law who, if you look closely, understands how a wine glass wrecks the neck. Spit hitting the ground in video art.

Film

Audible

The camera panned up away from our conversation and fixed on a cloud which artfully just fitted in the frame. It smouldered. The camera must have been mooring slowly following the cloud because the cheek of skyscraper sliced the cloud for a moment. It's actually half way. Is this narration? I was running a marathon. At the half-way point we coughed up the last part of the rent. I won't be able to afford the registration fees! Pathetic, I wound my watch, slowly, to linger in the space, and lived peacefully in my apartment for ages. There was a cup of tea and Zoë with her feet up on the windowsill. A carbon copy of the midnight sky – deep Goya neckline or my nap alarm in the morning which reminded me of the credits: opaque light spreading up from her neck, an unmistakable *V*. It was the title. Each letter smokily appearing, crystallising, clear, then evaporating again until the white title exited and we settled in, turning our phones off.

The Swirling Fonts

Swirling fonts of emotion adhered to her face sleeping, no doubt. I knew it, as did our friends who were beside us. How it didn't tickle we won't know. Cut, I said, my heart quickening. There was an audible relief, a billboard dropped on a story. Characters close in a café complaining about the pastry's texture. Hair on my arm replied easily in sans serif can we have a protagonist? Removing his ear hair during the sleeping scene metaphor. The crowd responded easily and the director said more! More!

Syndromes and a Century*

Don't star/t anything. Keep your _and
on a pencil the film will follow. Lift
your arms. French for the snack of water
from your reach into your bubbling brain.
Here is a limb-tangent. Get on the level.
Open your eyes – feeling. Corridor

the open shoe lace. Clip chips that peal
from your tennis indoors – those little squeaks.
Upright pain. Panda/Pandora – no matter.
We eat inside Jeff Koons' bubble gum

rare eclipse. It's a sensitivity
caused self-protection. Don't doubt it.
Don't begin. Film ¾ of the custard colonised
door, no less. Cutlery tides, waterfall tricks. A
lover buys her lover clothes. They never fit.

Mundane History

I was scratching a timber tabletop to a cold butter when the research at the fold of the season deflated into a breakfast basket right on the point of the blizzard. The water glass left an insignia on the corner of the table which way is the restroom? She ordered juice and was directed to the outdoor tables. I was with a ribbon of butter along the way (the code) of my keys. It went like sunset on her burger followed on from the depth of the bright ripe drink she left in the car. People were with a heel of bread, at best. I thought they had the tail of the Indian pickles and were injured switching the two, like the terrible lava lamp impact on an otherwise cordial gathering. Count the soup! Ring the chicken chips! The dish they brought out was diverse and agog mop salesman and women wiped the smirk off the face of the Japanese caption like a swimming breadth. Breath. In one. And he drilled into fishing nets with the ball of rubber bands the size of his own hen. They wanted to eat it. One table after another, and in rotation. A slow art. He translated. We got a chunky stew.

Misdirected

He twice answered the wrong question, assuming too much

displayed on the east side of time/pencil, east of name

dripping. Sand in my toes. She enjoyed the silence it caused,
wiggling. His wife's clothes which she would grow out of tailored
trousers she'd carry in her arms to the cliff and would be

interrupted risk. Falling. The film would fail. A portion of it

misdirected.

Ned Rifle

It was discovered *inform* her pottery which she made unknown to the file of army offices lined the dunes outside her window. They wore trees and had their faces made up by the night reflected in deep curry, though it was really more a ditch. It was hard to fall asleep. They rallied and marched like estate agents with a camera that gave to sleep eventually and made a dreaming sort of salad, day old, flopped on an ear. We feared the immaculate light of microscope evenings and what it did to us on the bus believing a pale orange timberish existence until midafternoon the train signals leaked on my meal ear I should say ear. Rifles shadowed on the walls shadows rifling through attention surely great big doubts head ache.

Unrelated

Reception blown about outside the textured masking
tape we used to hold the dash in place, a micro essay.

Place as assiduous assumptions after alarm. One leaf
mint misspelled mind in transcription, new chocolate

iceblock. Stupid goalie snorted the striker's
whiskers in a dare sneeze pinstripe, popular!

Olives

The representation of fortitude interested abalone leapt three pillows ate quickly by the cattle, their hard bellies. Vets corrected over scars on scientific dilettantism up to the elbows. Reached for the lower doorbell. Interrupted the plagiarist in feathery bushes, in 100 m sprint pre-gun posture bombsquad. Cardio artifice lightning bolt insignia pulled furtive Porsche blinker on the slow-motion highway replay – at least. Two seconds between blinks and nothing terrible at an eagle's weather. I put it in my hat. Imported doubt and India disintegrates some dumb economical haiku stricture. Olive olive she said and I responded affectionately. An orphan huddle-d to the margin in graphic design.

Spotless

To try and write say like Mallarmé ah malted tie anodyne or write it. I had a notice envelope inside and I went into the kit. The bag had an antidote to my own, or own poem, which was pronounced ownp. Ownp up an unlatch in tea, int. an assertion. I went up to it. Parked. The quarter poked out. I played embarrassed Joel Barrish in that garish genre Montauk cop character and gaudy. Twofold chalked up Twombly touched a back step on Sol LeWitt photography. Secretly new noticed. Entities. At a quarter past three I went. Ahem. A religious repetition. 4/10 of an anecdote intended, the rest a consequence interred troubled dream. Folding chair quantity. Endangered try. (We do dupe.) In the third person wore a coat in weather. Aunt. We go into the ligament of a family brush. Her out couch cushion!

Bob Dylan's Memory

A bus the way of a dolphin slipped through the used cars
electrical company

Employment was plain flour

Pancake into the months, or his leather jacket
pasted on the theatre's faces Johnny Ray

ray. The actual ambience, ambient light – amber
comes off the wireless e.g. to do your hair to, or

bluecaps

A voice in the air, piercing, or a collar made of cream
licking it off the patron's neck, little satin club

handheld memory, jagged, in through the
curtains sleeping most of the morning a freestyle wrist

arriving at the signature

A Sitting

Preface

I was sitting by the seaside absolutely, and ordering lemon water, and
the memory of coddled-egg sandwiches was sitting at the theatre café
indigestion mistaken for text message caused me to stay, hesitant of large
moves the fridge, three-seater couch (this when I *hesitated* that muscle.
Showtune melody, verse, refrain, *pulled* that muscle). I held my car to the
croissant and the sea crashed in writing the green wave hiccupped
    messily on
the sun bather or the beach umbrella opened in a reddy yellow gaudy
    bullfight.

Afterword

Sand castles toppled and the subtle moat broke up before the advent of
photography.

Wild Thing

Tidying up the rain her rusty hair leapt to an impartial towel and walked off the highway dreaming into traffic headlights her pale nudity ingenious, grieving. I helped clear chest crackles like trying to crush a coke can in the theatre. Could feed the dream beside her above a candle air atmosphere researched the eyes leaping or kept to the ceiling of the night's deeper dream, dream two, waking in the supermarket of the reef where the type bloodied and pooled causing surreal light protests attended meekly in our only suits. If you hover at the room long enough the silver scarves undressing in Leonard Cohen's semi-autobiographical novel swarmed against the very sled of her dream – woke up. The room was black bubbles atop ale crackling. I'm still breathing beside you lovey ivory hangers whispered. Thoughts rise like a chair lift. 'It's time for tea now', Bishop. And this, as in sleep, is also a romance. We play characters dissolve into chance. Futures like long towels cat clean between our dressing selves and crisp addresses are creamy screens we watch movies on. Cadillac Man. Uncle Boonmee/Buck.

The Impulse Story

Say everytime it's the classic jazz poem's repeat. And you
have it. Everyday everynight, the late era right on the cut
lip of embouchure. Bursting indiana jones boulder or, better,
white men can't jump jazz basketball pushed the drummer
sweated and we repeat *sweat*, too, refusing words such as *rivulet*.
Toms were a mess and he was fired. Had to walk home with his
sticks having sold his kit at a late-night broker plastered up to the
armpit. Bouncer came in gently but the torn brass couldn't
handle it. In jazz poems you can walk with a broken leg. Let's
mention Coltrane. Alice Coltrane's technicolour genius admin-
istered the choir who revised the 20th century in a sax dream
cast up to the elbow which she'd found congealed in sticky room-
light in one of those overpriced new york jazz bars you order
only one drink at. Ever tiny squeak squawk sips woke up next
day with the waitress' glare itch skips jazz the ultimate forgive-
ness. And you can just end it anywhere.

Video

There is no appetite for a novel of a certain kind, a window above curtains in hindsight we near the epiphany of the udder's

jungle. In private we admit to appropriate woeful entertainment watch it in kind thoroughly above curtailed high-art weariness.

Withstand the appetite for the novel we certainly kindle the abhorrent churlishness of epiphany, epigram.

The Green Ray

I can't believe I've been living my life at the edge of Rohmer who had been trickling along beside me at the pace of a novel. You can sit, really, and turn to the left or even lie back propped on your elbows and follow along the dialogue. And yet, there is so much to see! A peeling painted insignia on a café window and a young man sitting inside. Paint is caramelised milk, as is the sunlight, which slides in across the picture with gentleness. It's about as bossy and presumptuous as the innocuous stream or canal which is Rohmer every year of my life up until two years ago. Other artists that had been going along like this, unknown to me? Breton. His novel *Nadja* which seemed to me published across the entire 20th century and also into the 21st century, immaculate. William Maxwell before I discovered *The Chateau,* was mentioned by another writer talking to yet another – the remark offhand, a fissure – and I took the time to look up the driveway which, in the text, was described as 'curved' but on the cover of the book it looked really like the driveway went between cypresses which was a trick in one of Rohmer's films beginning with a camera settled on a wooden gate, a car, two women arriving – holiday – windows that fold in and shutters that go outways offering a glimpse of a bare bottom or something to move the plot along. You absorb the films, as you might literature. An almost inaudible hum of pleasure. It's almost not there and at times if the mind had wandered erasing parts of a paragraph, or dialogue had run on. You could sink to boredom but any concentration brings that sleepy pace back. All this on the L-shape of an elbow which grew itchy. This after nearly forty years! I rolled over onto one side and could see a couple tangled in the grass on the other bank. In my memory the water bubbled and was clear in parts but was more a deepening cape-like cobalt blue. It was late in the day.

Apichatpong Epochal

the film described as flicks on the imagination's
link by the great zip of the double helicopter

The Whole Sentence Was a Joke

The stones that made the alleyway bluestone or blackboard blue and chalk from the portion of the sky, shaped by the apex of a two-storey house's red roof bleached buzzy chalky metaphor. I stared down that bluestone alley and my eyes caught against newly painted aqua. Timber awnings – actually, lost in a thought about a poisonous leaf – painted the official colour of the North, Hanoi, where every new paint job, house or street, government or private, was a natural thin aqua. I removed my camera, felt around the lens and placed my fingers on its tyre-tread dimples, leaned against graffiti – silvery pink

– and shot the brilliant coriander.

Acknowledgements

Poems in *Aqua Spinach* were published in *Best Australian Poems 2017*, *China Australia Writing Centre Anthology*, *Cordite Poetry Review*, *Flash Cove*, *Foam:e*, *Island*, *Meanjin*, *Overland*, *Pink Cover Zine*, *Plumwood Mountain* and *Rabbit*. Thank you to the editors.

The titles of some of the poems are taken from films by Joanna Hogg, Apichatpong Weerasethakul, Yorgos Lanthimos, Luis Buñuel, Éric Rohmer, Stanley Kubrick, Anocha Suwichakornpong, John Ford and Hal Hartley.

Aqua Spinach was completed as part of a Doctorate in Creative Arts at the Writing and Society Research Centre, Western Sydney University. Wholehearted thank you to Kate Fagan and Chris Andrews for their expertise and editorial guidance.

I'm grateful to have such a sensitive, generous and skilled publishing team. Thank you to Emily Stewart for your editorial precision. Thank you also to Nick Tapper, and much gratitude to Ivor Indyk for your ongoing commitment to my writing.

Thank you to Apichatpong Weerasethakul for the image on the book's cover. Gratitude to Leo Charney for permission to use a section from *Empty Moments: Cinema, Modernity, and Drift* (Duke University Press, 1998). Also, thanks Toshiyuki Hasegawa and Philip Colley.

Thanks and love to Zoë and Ari.

These poems were written on the land of the Wurundjeri people of the Kulin nation. I pay my respects to their elders past and present.

The Giramondo Publishing Company acknowledges the support of Western Sydney University in the implementation of its book publishing program.

This project has been assisted by the Commonwealth Government through the Australia Council, its arts funding and advisory body.